The Really Easy Brass Series
General Editor: John Ridgeon

The *Really* Easy Trumpet Book

Very first solos for trumpet/cornet in B♭
with piano accompaniment

Christopher Gunning & Graham Lyons

© *1987 by Faber Music Ltd*
First published in 1987 by Faber Music Ltd
3 Queen Square London WC1N 3AU
Music drawn by Lincoln Castle Music
Cover illustration by Penny Dann
Cover design by M & S Tucker

Faber Music Limited
London

Contents

Preface

You need only be able to play a few notes on the trumpet (or cornet) to make music. The 15 little pieces in this book have been written with beginners in mind, but within the technical limitations this imposes there is plenty of scope for musical interest. The pieces are arranged progressively, so as well as musical satisfaction you can have the pleasure of hearing the step-by-step improvement in your playing. The piano accompaniments have been kept as simple as possible.

First Book of Trumpet Solos and *Second Book of Trumpet Solos* by John Wallace and John Miller are also available.

1. Lullaby

G.L.

2. Journey's End

G.L.

3. Miles Away

G.L.

4. Merry-go-round

G.L.

5. On Parade

G.L.

6. Up the Wooden Hill

C.G.

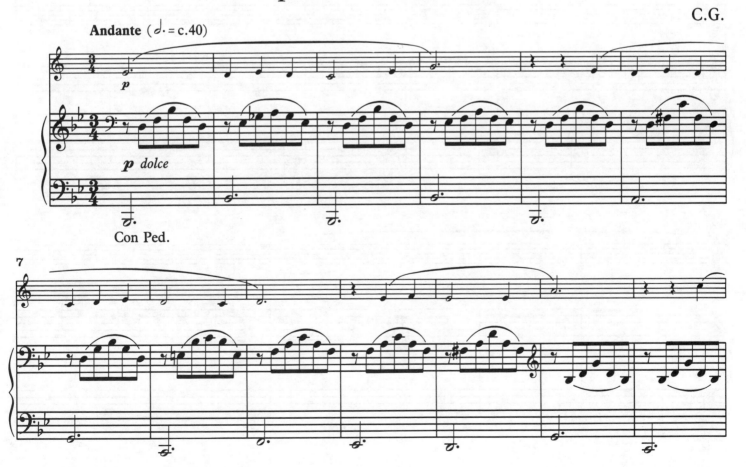

poco rit.   a tempo

7. Steam Special

C.G.

8. Promenade

G.L.

Ped. _____

9. Pigalle

C.G.

10. Aubade

G.L.

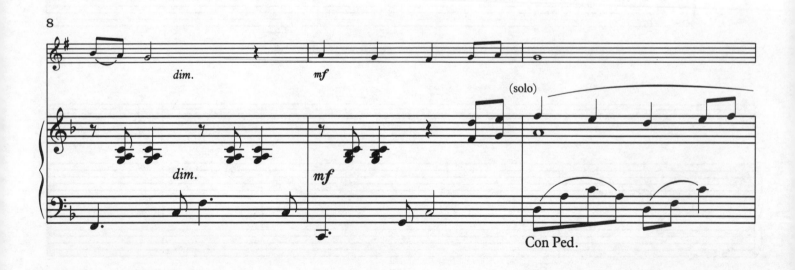

11. All Aboard

C.G.

21

12. Shepherd's Delight

C.G.

13. Royal Procession

C.G.

14. Driftwood

C.G.

15. March of the Tin Soldiers

C.G.

Printed by
Halstan & Co. Ltd., Amersham, Bucks., England